8 THINGS TO DO WHEN YOU TURN 20

8 THINGS TO DO WHEN YOU TURN 20

DEBOTOSH CHATTERJEE, IRS

An imprint of
Srishti Publishers & Distributors

Srishti Publishers & Distributors
A unit of AJR Publishing LLP
212A, Peacock Lane
Shahpur Jat, New Delhi – 110 049
editorial@srishtipublishers.com

First Published in India by
Blue Rose Publishers in 2022

First Published in India by Launchpad,
an imprint of Srishti Publishers & Distributors in 2024

CONTENTS

INTRODUCTION

This book is NOT meant to serve as a prescription pill for the readers. Instead, it aims to open up the minds of those who are in their 20s, and elaborates on some useful approaches towards life.

It has been my understanding that 21st century youth in India has much to achieve and conquer in the years to come. However, what often goes missing, is a bit of handholding in the formative years.

This book is my sincere attempt at extending a helping hand to the youth of this country, who are in their 20s, so as to make their futures better and brighter. Through this book, I have attempted to crystallise several life lessons into simple words and tried to highlight the common pitfalls of life. After all, it is always better to learn from the mistakes of others so that you do not waste time making the same mistakes yourselves.

The book is thus written as an "appetiser" which would stimulate the minds of the readers to be curious for more ideas in the right directions.

Chapter 1

Earn a Living. Be Atma-nirbhar

"The whole secret of existence is to have no fear. Never fear what will become of you; depend on no one. Only the moment you reject all help are you freed."

Swami Vivekananda

We live in a culture where self-reliance is still not considered to be a priority in teenage or early twenties. It is commonplace to see young people entirely dependent on their parents' income till their late 20s and even into early 30s. Mostly, "higher education" is cited as a credible reason for such dependence.

However, such dependence comes at a cost. Financial dependence on parents keeps your mental autonomy crippled. It works like slow poisoning, and by being dependent on your parents under the "cover" of education, you let your decision-making muscles atrophy.

Indian culture idolizes parents-kid relationship (which is very correct in a certain way, but NOT in this context) and thus finds nothing wrong with such dependence. This creates a social approval for such slow poisoning. This has led to a situation where we find "highly educated" persons in their late 20s and early 30s who hold numerous "degrees", but have no clue whatsoever about how to survive a single day without depending on parents!

It is always advisable to understand the concept of "self-reliance" from a very early age. It is not just about earning a living but about being the captain of your own life. In Western countries, it is commonplace to see college students working odd jobs at restaurants and bookshops to earn their monthly remuneration. Such jobs are frowned upon in India, and instead, a large section of the society incentivises a dependent existence for the youth in their 20s.

However, with the rising share of the working-age population and the crisis in the job market, India finally seems to have woken out of this societal slumber. Gone are the days when one would just clear an entrance test, enter a college and be assured of a certain type of job. The uncertainties in the economy are forcing changes in the education system and the mindset of 21st-century Indian youth.

The growing popularity of the social networking website LinkedIn in recent years among college undergraduates testifies to this observation.

The time spent in college is priceless. You may not

realise it in your 20s, but 10 years later, you will fully understand the quality of time that college years have made available to you. This is the period when the typical Indian boy or girl starts feeling the essence of "autonomy". Barring a few exceptions, most newbies in college actively seek a "college experience".

This is the time when you are like a free bird – there is no one to question your sleeping hours, eating habits or your social company. This would indeed be priceless autonomy if only there was no dependency on your parents for the monthly expenses. Bang! That's the biggest roadblock!

Thankfully, with the Internet revolution sweeping the country in the last five years, the Internet is now more accessible than ever. And with the Internet, a host of income opportunities become available. Content writing/editing, graphic designing, video editing, mobile app development, and digital marketing are some of the part-time jobs that have been thrown open to Indian youth in the last few years.

The good thing with such opportunities is that there is no "stigma" attached to such jobs, unlike being an errand boy at a bookshop or restaurant. What you earn through such jobs may not make you a millionaire in quick time (although such millionaires do exist), but it will tremendously boost your sense of self-worth and propel you on the road to progress.

Self-reliance is especially important in the context of

the uncertain world that today's youth are going to face. Changes which took hundreds of years to happen are nowadays happening in decades and years – population rise, internet user base, and ed-tech revolution can be considered in this context.

Such changes can be brutal, as has been duly highlighted by the COVID-19 pandemic. This creates the need to be prepared for contingencies which have the potential to blow away your life in one stroke.

In your 20s you should develop the concept of "being prepared" for contingencies – these are events/ phases/issues of life which are unexpected and uncalled for. You may have to bear the loss of loved ones, the loss of employment, or some other form of heartbreak. None of these events can be anticipated, but it is important to create some "mental insurance" against such possible calamities.

This does not mean I am forcing on you a pessimistic outlook towards life. Instead, I am only suggesting that life is not always fair, and the majority out there mostly face the unfair side of life. That's the reality we need to be prepared for!

This concept of self-reliance is now at the centre of the governance agenda for India. The COVID-19 pandemic has merely accentuated the need to prioritise self-reliance. India, as a country, is now seeking to be self-reliant more than ever. However, such a grand dream of national self-reliance can only be fulfilled when every youth understands the importance of this term in his or her own life.

Actionable Advice – If you are 20 and above, start generating some income for yourself right away. Make use of the Internet and start with any part-time job or paid internship.

Chapter 2

Time is More Valuable Than Everything Else

It is not enough to be busy. The question is: What are we busy with?

Henry David Thoreau

For the majority in their 20s, time is the most neglected asset. Years later, we realise the value of lost time but are unable to do anything about such loss. During college, most students focus over-enthusiastically on certain specific aspects of their future. They mostly focus on the following questions:

1. How much money will I earn?
2. What kind of car will I buy?
3. What kind of house will I live in?
4. What kind of person will I marry?
5. What kind of impression do I make on those around me?

This is what the overwhelming majority of youth

think in their 20s. And there is nothing fundamentally wrong with their thinking.

From an early age, Indian kids are taught about getting educated to get a job, buy a car and a house, get a good spouse and be "set" for life. These are generally the stereotypical ideas put inside our minds till the time we enter college.

But, the one thing nobody teaches us is the value and importance of "time". We stay blind to its importance until the point where we are drowned in EMIs, surrounded by family problems and stuck in jobs with no satisfaction.

Time is the most critical element for any human being. And yet, we neglect it as if we are going to exist forever. Have you ever considered this – by sleeping for 8 hours a day and working in an office for 8 hours a day for 75 years (an average life span), you will be spending almost 1/3rd of your life sleeping and another 1/3rd of your life in the office. That means office + sleep will occupy 50 years of your life, assuming you live till 75!

Have you ever thought this way? Most likely NOT. Because Indian kids are not taught to think in terms of time but in terms of other elements like money, family, assets, etc. The moment we start thinking in terms of time, our entire perspective towards life is jolted. For example, if you spend 8 hours working in a job which you hate, that means you will waste 25 years of your life simply hating your own existence. Is that sustainable?

That is why it is important to "think in terms of time" from a very early age. Time is the ultimate master – it decides literally everything! The act of working for an institution for a fixed salary (which appears to be the ultimate goal of life) is basically a transaction in which you trade your time and energy for a fixed sum every month. The modern-day term for salary, i.e. "compensation", has its roots in this transactive motive.

Whether you are still pursuing a college education or have transitioned into professional life, it is vital that you let people around you know that you value your "own" time. However, I am not suggesting any kind of ascetic, monk-like lifestyle full of hardships.

The crux of the argument is just that you respect your "time" on Earth. If you don't, life will make you realise the mistake a decade or two down the line.

Actionable Advice:

1. You should always put a premium on "your time". Don't put it out for sale or rent very cheaply.
2. Don't commit to any activity without fully realising its time commitments. Once time is gone, it never comes back.
3. Account for every hour of your life, and see how it magically propels you towards praiseworthy goals.
4. Get paid for your time, not your degrees or resume. You will be far richer than your peers that way!

Chapter 3

Acquaintances versus Friends – Know the Difference

Many people will walk in and out
of your life, but only true friends
will leave footprints in your heart.

Eleanor Roosevelt

College is perhaps that phase of life when 'friends' acquire gigantic importance in our lives. Bollywood teaches us about the 'yaarana' of college very passionately. Newcomers in most colleges, sooner or later, start getting into groups based on their mutual likes and dislikes.

If you are not a part of any group, people take you for a loner. So everybody wants to look 'cool' and get associated with a group. These group members exert tremendous influence on the way an individual thinks, speaks, eats, moves, and fights. Someone had said, "You are the average of the five people you interact with the most". This is exactly what happens in college.

In college, you will often hear phrases like 'Friends for life', 'Ye Dosti Hum Nahi Todenge' and so on. And yet, an average individual hardly communicates with more than one or two peers from his college after a span of 10 years.

What does this mean? It means the people whom we had so affectionately called "friends" during college were nothing more than acquaintances! They just happened to be in the same college at the same time that we were in. And they had some mutual commonalities. That's it!

Yet, the average college goer decides most of his college life based on suggestions, opinions and thoughts of their 'friends'. That's the problem.

Consider the following questions:

1. Which career to choose?
2. Should I go for higher studies or take up a job immediately after college?
3. Is it worthwhile to spend my parent's money on some particular coaching institute?
4. Is it wise to badger my parents for money to buy the latest iPhone in the market?

An average youngster answers such questions not on the basis of wide research and sound logic but on the basis of what his 'friends' are thinking and saying. Usually, they fall for the opinions of the one who looks the coolest in the gang and has a lot of followers. And that is clearly dangerous.

Five years down the line, we are stuck with a life that is based on the influence of someone with whom we are not even communicating. They have flown out of your life just the way they came in. They were acquaintances, not friends.

In my own experience, I was more or less a loner during my college years. I did not hang out with any of the "cool" gangs in college – these gangs had their own ways of having fun and their own set of stories to share. I could never be a part of these groups because of two reasons:

1. I could never compulsorily subscribe to their mode of thinking – if you are in a group, you always tend to think alike during the formative years of life.
2. I was an introvert by nature and, hence, did not have much incentive to go against my nature.

So, while my entire batch in college seemed to be busy with conventional ways of life, I could never live up to those standards. While my peers were busy firming up their job/academic prospects during college, I was troubled by the realisation that I could never get myself to work as a Chemical Engineer or any kind of engineer ever in my life!

It had taken me some time to come to this conclusion, but when I did, I could never go back to becoming a "good student" in college. Hence, I always stood out as an outlier. And I had nothing extraordinary about myself, either. I just did what I believed would take me somewhere where I wanted to be.

I had figured out that I would aim for the prestigious UPSC Civil Service Examination the very year I graduated from college. To fulfil this goal, I stuck to the boring and unconventional (and apparently pointless) job of reading two to three newspapers a day.

Besides, I took up odd jobs in content writing and content editing online to develop my writing skills. Remember, this was way back in 2012-13 when 1 GB of data of 3G internet used to cost 250 bucks! Some of my peers used to find it hilarious when I mentioned that I had to spend 750 bucks every month for 3G internet just to be a content writer! Most people around me had no idea what content writing was.

They found it even more hilarious when I used to mention that I used to get paid at the rate of 20 paise for every word I wrote. Clearly, I was not cut out for any of the fun groups around me!

In hindsight, this has been the biggest boon of my life. The 4 years in college which I spent exploring life in my "own" way were irreplaceable. The sense of self-worth that I got my "earning" @ 20 paise per word was exhilarating. The monthly earnings were meagre but immensely fulfilling.

Actionable Advice:

1. Do not consider 50% of your college to be your 'friends'. Usually, there will hardly be 4 or 5 people in the entire college who will be your 'real

friends' and remain a part of your life even after college.

2. Try to dedicate more of your energy to finding these real friends instead of wasting your college life 'flowing' with a hundred acquaintances.

Chapter 4

Stay Out of Herd Mentality

The opposite of courage is not cowardice; it's conformity. Even a dead fish can go with the flow.

Jim Hightower

This follows like a natural corollary of the previous point. If you know the difference between a friend and an acquaintance, you will most likely stand out of the herd mentality. If not, you will definitely be a part of the crowd.

Stepping into the 20s, the typical middle-class youth feels a surge of energy and enthusiasm. New people, new friends, new activities and entirely new dimensions of life open up before us. However, this is also the time when we easily fall prey to "trends" and "fashion".

We tend to goad ourselves to follow trends so as not to feel left out. Once imbibed, this habit of following trends becomes a "sticky" habit and is menacingly difficult to get rid of.

In college, most students persevere to fall in line with trends. These may be trends in career, thoughts, food, choice of friends, and a list of other things. Our decisions in the 20s are determined mostly by what we see around us. We desperately seek to be part of a "group". This is exactly the opposite of what you should ideally strive for in your 20s!

In reality, this is the age to develop "individuality". This is the right time to become a "maverick". In colloquial terms, you should be "Zara hatke". This is important in two ways.

For your own sake, you have to develop the courage to craft your own unique personality. That is the way in which you can grow into someone who is valued for his uniqueness in the job market.

For society's sake, it is mostly these mavericks who have redrafted the rules of living and changed the way in which humans look at certain aspects of life. Think about what world we would be living in today if mavericks like the Wright Brothers, Edison, Graham Bell, Steve Jobs and Dhirubhai Ambani had simply chosen to do what others around them were doing!

Western societies have created dedicated schemes and ecosystems to nurture such mavericks in large numbers who can improve the overall quality of life with their creativity and innovation. In India, such a culture was missing for a long time – thanks to the obsession with socialism and the bureaucracy-led growth model.

However, recently, the country has woken up to the need for an ecosystem that incentivises creativity and uniqueness. The rising tide of start-ups and an increasing number of Indian Unicorns stand proof of this change.

As someone in their 20s, you should know that the job market is gradually moving into a phase where those without unique skills and ideas would find it difficult to survive. In a way, this has forced youngsters to think out of the box in order to survive this reality. Such "out of the box" thinking should be the norm rather than the exception.

It is in the 20s that the human mind is at its agile best. If you burden it with useless trends, needless gossip and an impractical sense of conformity, your mind will soon give up. Thus, it is very important to keep your "mind" alive.

Benjamin Franklin once said, "Many people die at 25 and are not buried until 75". This is exactly what happens when you drift with the herd instead of taking command of your life.

Actionable Advice: Start thinking as an "individual", not as a member of a family, college or group. That will help you express your unique skills.

Chapter 5

Capitalism is Good - Realize and Augment Your Value

Doing well is the result of doing good. That's what capitalism is all about.

Ralph Waldo Emerson

India, for a long, was obsessed with Socialism and its perceived benefits. That obsession resulted in India having to beg to international agencies like World Bank in 1991 to save her economy.

Thankfully, those days are past now, and, as a nation, India seems to be discovering the perks of capitalism. This explains the entire emphasis on entrepreneurship, and pro-business steps taken by the government in the last few years.

However, as with self-reliance, the concept of Capitalism and its intended benefits for a country like India will not be fully understood unless the individual youth appreciates it properly. For a young student just stepping into college, concepts of Capitalism and Socialism do not make much practical sense.

Besides, given the sweeping influence of Left-wing thoughts across a major chunk of India's higher education centres, it is very natural for college-goers to feel a repulsion towards Capitalism. That's fine! Except, when you evaluate Capitalism on its merits in the context of your own life, you can see through certain truths.

If you have understood the concept of "self-reliance", you will also understand that Capitalism is the fundamental philosophy that underpins man as a self-reliant being instead of merely being part of some unit. Without getting into the nitty-gritty of the pros and cons of Capitalism, it can be convincingly asserted that, up to a certain point, this philosophy strongly supports and advocates individual empowerment.

Let's understand this with an example. Imagine that you want to earn some pocket money during your college days. For this, you decide to create a gaming app for Android mobile phones. How would you like to earn from your efforts on this mobile app? Do you want a group of inaccessible people sitting somewhere in Delhi to decide the price of your creation using some opaque and obsolete method? Or do you want the best possible price for your product under the present circumstances?

Of course, you would love to get the best possible price. That is exactly what Capitalism does. It creates an ecosystem in which skills and efforts are rewarded proportionately.

Yes, the system does have its flaws, like any other

institution. However, Indian youth in their 20s need to understand that instead of bashing any philosophy based on limited theoretical understanding, they should focus on the practical benefits in their own lives. If they aspire to be self-reliant, they need an ecosystem which remunerates the right skills at the right time. That's how a society grows!

Like it or not, you live in a time when you will have the biggest stake in deciding your own value to the world. This is the generation of the "self-made man". In the Bollywood blockbuster movie
"Super 30", which is based on the life of the Mathematics prodigy Anand Kumar, the protagonist says:

"Ab raja ka beta raja nahi banega. Raja wahi banega jo haqdaar hoga".

(Now, the son of a king won't become the king by default. Only those rightfully deserving will become the king).

This succinctly summarises the entire argument in a single sentence.

Chapter 6

Learn to be a Lifelong Learner

Wisdom is not a product of schooling but of the lifelong attempt to acquire it.

Albert Einstein

One of the biggest problems with Indian education culture is that we are taught to get our education so as to stop further education! Isn't that an irony, a paradox and a ridiculous idea all at the same time? Yes, but it's true.

Why are you told to get into a college? Why are you told to go for higher education? The prevailing narrative in our country is that you get educated to get a job and stop having the need for further education!

This is exactly the reason we are stuck with a workforce whose major chunk is unemployable. In a fast-changing world, employment parameters change from time to time. This means that people who depend solely on their formal school and college education in their professional lives often find themselves to be outdated and irrelevant some years down the line.

Imagine a person who wanted to spend his life repairing radios. Or someone who wanted to be a lifelong clerk at a bank. Or someone who has never bothered to learn anything beyond manual accounting at a local shop. How easy do you think their lives are today?

This is where the role of "education" (in the real sense) comes in. Your college, especially, should teach you (actively and passively) that you have to remain a learner and a student throughout life. And that such lifelong learning is not a punishment but a fruitful investment to get the best out of your own existence.

Sadly, Indian higher education appears to be light years away from being capable of effectively communicating this idea to the youth. Hence, the onus is on the person concerned to get self-educated.

The economic devastation caused by COVID-19 has somewhat highlighted the need for this self-education. "If you have to survive, you better keep learning" – this is perhaps the message that Mother Nature is sending us through this pandemic.

Large-scale job losses and restructuring in companies during the pandemic have led to fundamental shifts in job requirements. A skill as basic as proficiency in Microsoft Excel may have been overlooked by employers 5 years back, but today, they would consider that skill to be mandatory for an engineering graduate to join their company. Your college may not have had a course on MS Excel, but if you need the job, you better learn it! That's how the world is going to painfully push you into a "learning attitude" if you don't learn it early on.

The tricky thing about this "learning attitude" is that it is excruciatingly painful to acquire in the later years of life. Unless this soft skill is imbibed in the formative years, it is very difficult to adapt and survive later on. Take a look at how difficult most people from our parent's generation find it to handle mobile apps and computers, and you will feel the essence of what I am saying.

Actionable Advice:

1. Make the best use of upskilling platforms like Coursera, edX and Udemy to keep your professional skills relevant and in shape.

2. Stay in touch with people who are in the field that you want to be in. They will give you a clearer picture of reality than anyone else. In simple terms, develop your "networking" skills.

3. Don't rely on outdated college curricula to magically get you to excellent jobs/projects. Help yourself with the necessary skills to get what you feel should be rightfully yours.

Chapter 7

The MOST Important Thing They Don't Teach Us – Financial Intelligence

Those who master money are free to serve others who are still mastered by it.

Orrin Woodward

Financial intelligence is perhaps one of the most neglected aspects of education in our country. We are taught science, mathematics, history, geography and whatnot. However, barring the very few who actually go for higher studies and research in these subjects, most people do not find their relevance in daily life.

After all, knowing about Vasco da Gama's voyages or India's ancient past would not exactly excite a middle-aged family man working a routine job to provide for his family. However, the one subject that has lifelong usefulness for every single individual that comes out of the education system is sadly nowhere in the curriculum.

That subject is: Basic Sense of Finances.

You must be aware of a certain Sushil Kumar from

Bihar who won Rs 5 crore prize money in the popular TV show Kaun Banega Crorepati in 2011 but was back on the streets in a few years.

Why do such cases happen?

Because of the lack of financial intelligence.

For the question 'How do you wish to get rich?', most college-goers would respond 'Winning a jackpot'. However, you can turn the pages of the Internet for an eternity and still not find the names of any of the millions of jackpot winners in the list of richest people in the world.

What makes you rich is not the wealth but the manner in which you put it to use. Wealth without planning can be an unmitigated disaster!

What do college graduates typically do?

(1) Get a job and feel overjoyed when they receive a salary.

(2) Spend the salary recklessly after meeting basic requirements of rent, household bills, etc.

(3) Within a year or two, they start 'dreaming big'. They take home loans and car loans. They may buy a home, a car, and all the latest gadgets out on the market. They may use their credit cards liberally. They try to "feel" rich.

(4) A few years down the line, they get bored and

disgusted with the job. But now they are stuck in the quagmire of loans and debt. Now, they work for the company, earn their salary, and also work for the bank by paying off their loans.

(5) By the time all the loans are paid off, the prime of their youth is already over. They willingly chose to remain chained to loan repayment cycles, whereas their time could have been better spent on more productive activities. Some call this the 'modern say bonded labour'.

What should you ACTUALLY do?

(1) Start saving your money as early as possible. It does not matter whether you are in school or college. Start saving 100 bucks from your pocket money every month from the age of 20. Increase the savings by 10% every year. Keep the money invested for long periods of time – 5, 10, 15, 30 years or maybe more. Thank me when the returns start pouring in.

(2) Understand the power of "compounding". Einstein had termed it the '8th wonder of the world'. Sadly, most of the young generation is unaware of this concept. The process of compounding is perhaps the best way to get rich within a reasonable frame of time.

(3) Invest in assets and NOT liabilities. Most of us have no clarity on the concepts of assets and liabilities while we are in college. Rich people invest in assets. Poor and middle-class invest in liabilities.

Assets add to your income, while liabilities take away your income. A house put on rent is an asset, but one in which you are living is not. The car that you drive is a liability. Your mutual fund portfolio is an asset – it will give you returns in the future.

In short, the best birthday gift is NOT a car/mobile phone/TV but a lumpsum deposit in a good mutual fund.

Must read books:
(1) Rich Dad, Poor Dad – Robert Kiyosaki.
(2) The Richest Man in Babylon – George S Classon.
(3) Master your Money, Master your Life – Abhishek Kumar

Chapter 8

Less Talk, More Action.
Be Solution-Oriented

No matter how hard or unfair life seems to be, we can overcome any challenge if we focus on finding solutions.

Brad Turnbull

In our 20s, we are bubbling with energy. "Action" comes easily to us. We are always ready to act. However, more often than not, our energy is misdirected to unnecessary activities during the 20s. This is because of the lack of awareness of the surroundings.

Moving from teenage to the 20s changes several aspects of our lives. The most important change is that the number of "variables" in life increases rapidly.

Before we enter college, our world is limited to academics, parents, siblings, relatives and friends. At this point, a typical middle-class teenager's life is free from major responsibilities. But this changes drastically once college begins and they creep into their 20s.

Consider these changes for example:

1. More friends and acquaintances.
2. Possible addition of the romantic angle in life.
3. Awareness about career and the growing sense of "doing something in life".
4. Parents growing old or retiring or falling sick.

These aspects of life were present in their lives earlier as well, but they were strongly subdued due to the protective cover of "childhood". As children, most middle-class youth were lucky enough to be shielded from such variables by their families. It is only in the 20s that a deeper understanding of these "variables" starts developing in the mind.

These are called the "variable" aspects of life because one cannot have complete control over these aspects. However, it is only the tiny minority of youth who manage to handle these variables efficiently and subsequently do well in life. The majority, on the other hand, gets entangled in a mess of problems which gradually become insurmountable with time.

Technically, in your 20s, you should fully understand the concept of handling the "variable" aspects of life. This understanding will be a lifelong asset and serve you well on multiple occasions. The way to handle these issues well is to develop a "solution-oriented mindset". This looks easy on paper but is incredibly difficult to practice in real life.

Consider the most typical example of a "problem" for

a college-goer in India. Halfway through his college life, he realises that he is on the wrong course, and he feels stuck! Such realisations in your 20s are extremely important as they help you figure out the nitty-gritty of life. However, the important thing is whether you are able to use such realisations to improve your life.

So, say you are stuck in the wrong course/degree/college at the age of 21. You feel that you have wasted 2 to 3 years of your life for nothing. How do you come out of it?

The majority actually does nothing. Yes, NOTHING. They simply go with the tide without taking conscious action and get further messed up by the complexities that the future throws up.

Not taking action to handle the variables of life slowly becomes an ingrained habit and becomes a part of your personality. This is the surest way to feel like a "walking dead" 10 or 15 years down the line.

A minuscule percentage of youth in their 20s, though, take action to work on their realisations and understanding at this age. They live life from "project to project". A "project" is anything in which you want a solution.

1. You are stuck in the wrong degree. So you start on the project to find a solution to make sure that you get the optimum from the years already "wasted", and thereafter chart your own career path. So, if you are stuck in Engineering (which

is the norm for millions of Indian youth today), you have to take a call on the future while you are in college. If you don't, you consciously start on the path of "walking dead".

2. Your financial condition is weak, and your parents may not be able to sponsor your future education. Once you have acknowledged this problem, don't just sit on it and whine like the majority tends to do.

Instead, work out your available options – Is an education loan available? Can you work part-time (online) to gather some money? Can you get help from someone else? A rational analysis of these options should give you a feasible solution to work with.

But this is easier said than done. And the majority, anyway, chooses the comfortable path of whining and cursing their own luck!

3. Your parents are not supportive and have a toxic attitude towards your higher education – this is very much possible in the case of girls in our country.

In such a situation, the youth can think about being self reliant and using her own income to the extent possible in financing her education. If not, she can ask for help from a friend/relative in the form of a loan which she would pay back after a certain period of time. Besides, the government is always coming up with schemes to help the youth in their educational avenues.

In the 21st century, you should not ruin your life just because your parents happened to have ruined theirs!

4. You have wasted aeons of time in a disastrous relationship and now feel hollowed out and empty. At such moments, life feels frozen, and the future appears meaningless in every conceivable way.

However, it is the "attitude" to look for solutions that help in times like these. Yes, you will not be able to magically turn your life around in a day.

But such an attitude will give you the fortitude to survive. It is this skill to survive and fight another day that the youth need to acquire.

These are typical problems that 20s people are bound to face at some point in time. When analysed by a neutral third person, all these problems have solutions. However, the real challenge is to see that solution in your own life and implement it.

Indian youth have somehow been led into thinking that life is about avoiding difficulties and problems at all costs. The prevailing narrative is that there should be no trouble in life. In reality, this is the surest prescription to invite trouble in your life!

Instead of living your life merely to avoid trouble, you should make it a conscious habit of tackling issues on their merit. This is because you can only control a few aspects of life, but the rest remain outside your influence.

Consider driving, for example. You can only control how "you" drive. You may be the best driver the world has ever seen, but you never know when some drunkard will come and slam his vehicle into yours and kill you. That is just not within your control.

Does this mean you should not drive at all? No, you should. But you should also know the reality of driving so that you don't stay in a bubble.

The same is the case with life. You can only "control the controllable(s)". When you try to control everything in life, you end up ruining it. Becoming superstitious is one such manifestation of life being ruined.

CONCLUSION

The main point in writing this book is not to show off my superior understanding of life. These are issues which most middle aged people may understand very freely. However, the key thing is to identify them early in life so that the well-known "traps of life" can be avoided.

It is in the 20s that one develops the foundation which sustains and enriches a person's future. As per the famous 80/20 Principle, 80% of the output in a process is because of 20% of its critical input. Hence, it is very important that for any process, we find that critical 20%, which will create the lion's share of the output.

If life is a process, that 20% input is to be found in the 20s. The way you live your life in your 20s will overwhelmingly determine how your life shapes up in the future.

If these precious years are wasted, and that too because of avoidable mistakes, then the best of efforts thereafter will not yield as much desirable output.